The Durán Madonna by the Flemish painter Rogier van der Weyden. Late Gothic 1435-1438.

HISTORY of ART 1

Guide for beginners

ARTHWR BASS

Digital Creative Publishing

Representation of Egyptian art. Painting on the wall of the tomb of the sculptor Ipuy. In this one it can be noticed the Egyptian adoration for cats. Ipuy appears with a small cat on his lap and there is another one under his wife's chair.

Editor-in-chief
Vanessa Lozada Gil

Author
Arthwr Bass

Design and layout
Digital Creative Publishing

Translation
Rafael Morón Abad
Digital Creative Publishing

Photographs
Royalty free images (FFCU images)
(Credits to the respective author in each image)

Cologne Cathedral, Germany. Example of Gothic style architecture. Construction began in 1248 and ended in 1880, it had a break in its construction of 350 years.

Dome of the Cathedral of Zamora. Example of galloned Romanesque architecture.

TABLE OF CONTENTS

Paleolithic

Neolithic

Age of metals

Primitive art

Art is the result of human creativity and expressiveness with a communicative or aesthetic purpose. The artist expresses his ideas, emotions or vision of the world using physical or sound resources. Like humanity, art has also evolved through time. Its development has been seen in different aspects such as genre, design, format, and style. Growing along with the changes in society and suffering just like the artists themselves, but surviving as it is an inevitable method of acculturation.

The object of study in History of Art is understood to be all types of expression through painting, sculpture, architecture, ceramics, furniture and other decorative objects. Although its study is less frequent, other fine arts such as music, dance, literature, goldsmithing and clothing are also analyzed.

Primitive art is the art developed by humans from the Stone Age (Upper Paleolithic, Mesolithic and Neolithic) to the Metal Age.

Paleolithic

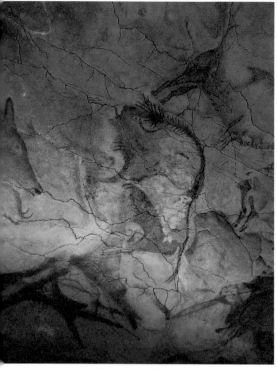

Painting in the Altamira cave, which is considered to have been occupied by different groups from 35600 to 13000 years ago.

The first objects created by humankind and the first artistic manifestation are credited to Homo neanderthalensis, some 65000 years ago, although the greatest prehistoric artistic findings date back to 25000 B.C. and were made by Homo sapiens in the Upper Paleolithic period.

The evolution of art throughout history is not like that of technology, since it does not accumulate its innovations as, for example, a manufacturing process would.

The location of these findings appears in Southern Africa, the Western Mediterranean, Central and Eastern Europe (Adriatic Sea), Siberia (Lake Baikal), India and Australia.

The Paleolithic period is considered to have lasted until the end of 8000 BC.

Objects for daily use

The first objects created by man were intended to meet a need, rarely adding a decorative, non-functional element. With them, they expressed their creativity and vision of the world. These were tools made of carved stone (flint, obsidian), bone or wood.

One of the most important references is the Altamira cave in the north of Spain where archaeological findings include: hand axes, points, javelins, scrapers, malacological remains (shells that were useful and food remains), ichthyofauna remains (fish bones), beads, pendants, mammal remains, needles, burins, plates, airbrushes and decorated animal scapulae.

Painting

In their context, Paleolithic individuals represented what they saw and lived in their paintings, concrete mimesis. These were representations created on the walls of the caves where they lived.

SINCE THEY ARE NOMADIC, THEY MOVE WITH THE SEASONS AND LEAVE CERTAIN SIGNALS FOR FUTURE NOMADIC GROUPS.

View of the ceiling of the Great Hall of Polychromes at Altamira, the Paleolithic masterpiece. Throughout the cave of Altamira, there are different styles of painting since its habitation took place over thousands of years and in non-continuous periods of time.

They gathered 70 to 100 individuals and lived in hordes, known today as clans or tribes. Generally, the chief was the one who led the hunt and who made the paintings.

In form, painting was primarily done on the ceilings of caves. The optical trigger of the painting is the loose and precise forms to see the figures at night and hear the matter. The figures looked static and had no order, although some scientists claim that the superimposition was intentional and that some paintings and engravings were intentionally placed as a form of composition.

The theme of Paleolithic paintings was 98% about animals and 2% about men.

The colors used in their paintings resembled the color of flesh and were: red, produced with iron oxide; black, with manganese oxide; and ocher, with clay. From the glaciations of 600000 B.C. it is believed that man already manipulated fire. By 15000 or 14000, the soot generated by fire was used to paint with the black color. Later, the colors blue and green appeared as a product of malachite and cobalt, yellow as a product of fats and secretions, and white as a product of crushed bones and other minerals.

Most of the painting done in the Paleolithic period is considered cave painting, which was developed for its magical-religious character and had a naturalistic sense where animals were represented. Magic was an important part of the culture of the Paleolithic groups and, for this purpose, they made art. They considered that all objects had a soul and made their paintings to have control over hunting, fertility rituals or ceremonies.

EVERYTHING THAT APPEARED IN THEIR PAINTINGS WAS NECESSARY; THERE WERE NO ORNAMENTS OR AESTHETIC ADDITIONS.

For individuals to paint inside the caves, they needed artificial lighting since natural light was insufficient. It is believed that they burned bones since the bone marrow functioned as fuel generating a large flame without smoke or odors.

Some of the most important references in the painting of this period are the Caves of Altamira (north of Spain), Tito Bustillo, Trois Frères, Chauvet and Lascaux, in the French-Cantabrian region.

Sculpture

Some groups of Paleolithic individuals made totems, animals or natural objects representing an animal, which identified the clan.

Venuses were predominant as Paleolithic sculptures. They were figures where femininity was represented with an exempt relief and as a symbol of fertility. The venus were figures of nude women generally carved in Paleolithic limestone and stained with red ochre. The forms were exuberant, voluptuous and unrealistic, since their abdomen, vulva, buttocks and breasts are extremely voluminous. At some point, it was thought that this was the ideal of beauty held by the Paleolithic tribes.

Paleolithic statuettes are small in size and are considered practical to be moved as they were nomadic. Most sculptures have been found deteriorated, with missing and damaged parts due to the transfers and time.

Some of the most important references are: the Venus of Willendorf, the Man of Brno, the Mammoth of Vogelherd and the Lady of Brassempouy.

Venus of Willendorf found in Willendorf (Austria), along the Danube, during excavations. The figure is 11 centimeters high, 5.7 centimeters wide and 4.5 centimeters thick with a circumference of 15 centimeters.

Music and dance

In ancient times, the essence of music and dance resided in their deep-rooted connection to various rituals and ceremonies that marked significant moments in human life. Music and dance had a ritual purpose to celebrate births, deaths, weddings, fertility, hunting or war. Prehistoric individuals modulated their voices to create melodious sounds and moved their bodies to express their feelings. Later, instruments were used to generate sounds. At their core, music and dance allowed prehistoric individuals to tap into the very essence of their emotions.

Neolithic

Paintings of the caves of El Cogul or Roca de los Moros located in El Cogul (Las Garrigas), Catalonia.

This period encompasses the years 8,000 B.C. to approximately 3,000 B.C. (3,500 Europe, 1,500 America and 8,000 Asia) and is also called the New Stone Age. It was initially called Neolithic because of the findings of polished stones that seemed to accompany the development and expansion of agriculture.

At this time, there was a profound change in the behavior of human beings, who ceased to be nomadic and became sedentary. The clans devoted themselves to agriculture and cattle raising, and new forms of coexistence and religion emerged. The knowledge of the human being expanded.

Some of the societies in the Neolithic followed the matriarchal model, and there were even vestiges of populations whose settlements followed the urban planimetry or organized housing model, for example in Tell as-Sultan (Jericho), Jarmo (Iraq) and Çatalhöyük (Anatolia). The first dwellings were made of wood and were raised off the ground to avoid humidity.

With the change of the human thinking about religion, funerary constructions or megalithic architecture creations appeared.

New materials appeared in this period, such as amber, rock crystal, quartz and jasper.

ART DURING THIS PERIOD ALREADY EXPRESSED SENSATIONS AND WAS OPEN TO THE ARTIST'S EXPERIENCES. UNLIKE PALEOLITHIC ART, IT WAS TRANSFORMED TO SHOW A STYLE THAT DID NOT FOCUS ON SHOWING REALITY AS IT WAS.

Instead of making figures faithful to the shapes of animals or human beings, in the art of this period we find ideographic and schematic signs that explain how the artists wanted to express an idea or concept, that is, they created symbols instead of simple images.

Painting

Fragment of a spear carved from reindeer antler. The details were made with a stone. The sculptor turned the bison's head 180 degrees to maintain the profile view.

In the Neolithic, art is schematic and the images work together in a way that tells a story.

The context is that they paint what they think.

Most of the drawings have an order similar to that followed at the time of plowing the fields in agriculture, stripes from left to right or, the other way around.

Neolithic painting of the Mediterranean arc showed the human figure in basic strokes. A man could be distinguished by the cross-shaped strokes and a woman, in the form of a triangle.

At this time, the bird's-eye perspective appeared in paintings, a perspective where it was drawn as if seen from above.

Some of the paintings presented thick red strokes as abstract and anthropomorphic signs with more dynamic compositions abandoning the fidelity of the Paleolithic.

During this period, cave painting was developed in the Iberian Peninsula, on the Mediterranean coast of Spain, where hunting scenes were depicted on rocks in the open air and human figures were schematically represented.

Some of the most important references are located in: El Cogul, Valltorta, Alpera and Minateda; North Africa (Atlas, Sahara), in the area of present-day Zimbabwe; and the Pinturas River in Argentina, especially the Cueva de las Manos (Cave of the Hands).

Pottery

Pottery is the art of making clay objects. This discovery was vital for Neolithic man as it allowed him to make vessels for storage or cooking, making his life much easier. Prior to the emergence of pottery, early humans relied on more rudimentary methods of container creation, such as weaving baskets or fashioning containers from natural materials.

Before this period, they used empty gourds, which could not be put on the fire, and wicker baskets, which could not contain water. Later, Neolithic man waterproofed the wicker baskets with sun-dried or fire-baked clay. Man learned to shape the clay with a wicker skeleton and later abandoned it to make clay-only pots. The shapes of these pots continued to be gourd-shaped and of similar dimensions.

The ceramics of the early Neolithic period were called cardial and were decorated with various types of incisions made with the fingers, punches or polished stone or bone spatulas. They were called cardial because these incisions were also made with shells of a mollusk called Cardium edule or cockle.

Neolithic art on a rock in Africa.

> HAVING POTS ALLOWED THE NEOLITHIC MAN TO BE FAR FROM WATER SOURCES OR TO AVOID MAKING MANY TRIPS TO GET WATER. HOWEVER, NOT ONLY WATER WAS STORED, BUT ALSO GRAINS, SEEDS AND GROUND PRODUCTS.

When supplies ran low, all they had to do was to travel and restock. Hunters preferred to carry wicker or woven pieces because they weighed less and were not fragile. Those who preferred clay pieces were the herders and farmers because it provided them with a safe place to store water and other products. When the methods of preserving meat were developed, humans no longer had to hunt on a daily basis..

Movable art refers to the type of art that is small in size and easy to move. The ceramics of mobiliary art were decorated with serrated edges and shell impressions. There are indications that suggest that the first forms of decoration were made with ropes that were also used as reinforcement. Other decorative elements that were added were the groove, cord (line in relief as a rope located slightly below the rim) and handles of different types.

Neolithic period vessel in China.

Textile art

Thanks to the invention of weaving, different types of clothing were developed to protect the body of Neolithic men and women. Sandals or espadrilles were very popular and were made with a fabric on the sole that followed the shape of the foot and had braided braces. The tunics took advantage of natural fibers such as wool.

Age of Metals

Bronze Age vessel. It is now in the National Museum of Ireland.

The Age of Metals is the period between approximately the 4th and 1st millennium B.C. It corresponds to the last phase of prehistory when humans discovered how to manipulate and melt metal to be molded, and began to use elements such as copper, bronze (alloy of copper and tin) and iron to create objects.

The Age of Metals is characterized by the development of a wide range of functional and precious metal objects, a significant increase in economic productivity, trade (initiated by the interest in the material of peoples lacking metal), exchanges and the consequent emergence of skilled workers, many of whom were involved in artistic activities, albeit of a semi-functional nature.

The use of metal manipulation was born in the Anatolian Peninsula from 5000 B.C., where the smelting of copper was discovered by chance when it fell into the fire.

In some earlier eras, certain communities developed jewelry and other objects with the help of metals, but it was not until a large number of objects were produced that it was called the Age of Metals.

THE AGE OF METALS IS DIVIDED INTO THE COPPER AGE OR CHALCOLITHIC (III MILLENNIUM B.C.), THE BRONZE AGE (II MILLENNIUM B.C.) AND THE IRON AGE (I MILLENNIUM B.C.).

Egyptian, Mesopotamian and Sumerian art emerged during the Bronze Age, and the pyramids at Giza, near Cairo in Egypt, were created during this time.

It should not be forgotten that humanity has not passed from one age to another at the same time all over the world, since its progress has not followed the same steps everywhere. Each continent has evolved at a different pace.

The Bronze Age flourished mainly in the Near East. As the Bronze Age came to an end around 1100 BC, the history of art reveals a widening gap between northern and Mediterranean Europe. Iron Age art developed mainly from the Mediterranean to as far as the British Isles.

Some of the representative tools of this period with decorative and ornamental designs are helmets, body armor, swords, spears, shields, fibulae, axe heads and other weapons.

Stonehenge. A megalithic monument of the cromlech type. It was built between the end of the Neolithic and early Bronze Age; how humans could move stones of such weight and size at that time is still a mystery.

Megalithism

At the beginning of the Age of Metals, the manipulation of metals was not so prominent in northern Europe, where megalithic constructions were erected at that time.

The Copper Age saw the rise of megaliths, stone funerary monuments or shelters consisting of one or more blocks.

Some types of megaliths are the dolmen, a large table made from stone slabs, the menhir, a long and erect stone in rough or minimally carved form, and the cromlech, a monument of stones inserted into the ground adopting a circular shape.

Other types of megaliths found in the Balearic Islands are the naveta, a monumental tomb in the form of a truncated pyramid, the taula, a construction whose central element is T-shaped, and the talayot, a tower with a covered chamber.

Some of the most important references are the magnificent Stonehenge stone complex; the megalithic temples of Malta (Ggantija, Hagar Qim, Mnajdra, Tarxien), which were developed between 5000 BC and 2500 BC on the islands of Malta and Gozo, and it is believed that fertility rituals and animal sacrifices were performed there. Given the size of the temples, the architectural technique used is surprising, as they are made entirely of stone on a clover-shaped base. When there were several temples together, a common wall was created for all of them.

The Thinker of Hamangia, sculpture found in Cernavoda, Romania created between 4000 and 3500 BC.

Sculpture and pottery

Ceramics became more elegant in design than in previous eras and a new range of ceremonial and religious artifacts began to emerge.

A particularly rare Bronze Age statue is the Palaikastro Kouros (1,480-1,425 BC), a chryselephantine sculpture carved from a hippopotamus tooth, found on the island of Crete.

Late prehistoric sculpture flourished during the Age of Metals, taking full advantage, for example, of bronze casting methods.

In some archaeological excavations carried out in the megalithic temples of Malta, clay statuettes with figures representing both men and women were found.

The best examples of Bronze Age sculpture appeared in the cradle of civilization around the Mediterranean, during the rise of Mesopotamia (present-day Iraq).

In the valleys where the Tigris and Euphrates rivers flow, several important civilizations flourished in the distant past: the Sumerians, Akkadians, Babylonians and Assyrians. This area was populated by two different races: the eastern Semitic Akkadians (later called Assyrians and Babylonians) and the Sumerians, whose land later was later known as Mesopotamia.

One of the most important references is the bell-shaped pottery developed by the settlement of Los Millares, Spain, during the Copper Age. These pottery pieces depicted schematic human figures with large eyes.

Painting

Bronze Age weapons from the Near East.

Examples of Bronze Age art within the Mediterranean area include a wide range of painted ceramics and fresco murals that include landscapes as well as figurative images of humans and animals. There were paintings dedicated to the gods, and a number of artistic tributes to kings and rulers were seen.

The art of the Bronze Age Mediterranean was a testament to the vibrancy and diversity of the cultures that flourished during this epoch. It reflected the deep connection between art and society, capturing the essence of religious devotion, cultural identity, and the hierarchical structure of power. These artistic creations continue to inspire and captivate.

Scandinavia has more than 30,000 sites where cave paintings depicting ships, animals and human figures painted during the Bronze Age have been discovered.

Mesopotamia

Ancient Egypt

America, Africa and Asia

Ancient art

History is said to begin with the invention of writing, and it is at this point that ancient works of art begin to be created. The invention of writing marked a before and after in the way human beings communicated, since it was necessary to express complex ideas in close relation to the sound of spoken language. This concept would encompass the first artistic manifestations of the majority of peoples and civilizations of all continents just at the time of the appearance of the corresponding writing.

The invention of writing is disputed between Egypt and Mesopotamia where it appeared contemporaneously in the Age of Metals, around the IV and III millennium B.C. The Sumerian, Indian and Mayan peoples also developed writing, each with different characteristics specific to their culture.

Writing is closely linked to art because it is part of the graphic representations of humanity.

Mesopotamia

Example of cuneiform script, an administrative account regarding barley malt and semolina entries.

At the beginning of the emergence of ancient art, the first great cities arose all over the world, mainly bounded by great rivers such as the Nile, the Tigris and Euphrates, the Indus and the Yellow River.

One of the most important advances of the time was the invention of writing, which was used to keep records of economic and commercial transactions.

Mesopotamia developed in the area between the Tigris and Euphrates rivers (present-day Syria and Iraq), where from the 4th millennium B.C. various Mesopotamian cultures and civilizations such as the Sumerians, Akkadians, Amorites, Assyrians, Chaldeans (of Babylon), Kassites and Hurrians succeeded one another. Later, with the fall of Babylon, the Persian Empire integrated Mesopotamia, Syria and Israel to its dominion in 539 B.C. and assimilated their artistic tradition, originating a creative art, but with foreign influences.

Writing

In Mesopotamia, the first written code called cuneiform writing was created around 3500 BC on clay tablets. It is called cuneiform because the signs were carved on the clay in the shape of a wedge. Mesopotamian writing was based on pictographic and ideographic elements.

THANKS TO THE EMERGENCE OF WRITING, LITERATURE DEVELOPED AND HUMANS WERE ABLE TO EXPRESS ALL THEIR CREATIVITY.

The Sumerians and Akkadians wrote about thirty texts with myths about divinities, among which the following stand out: the descent of Inanna to hell and the myths generated around the gods Enki and Tammuz. There is also the poem Lugal ud melambi Nirpal (The works of Ninurta), whose content is didactic and moral.

One of the most important references of Sumerian literature is the Poem of Gilgamesh, from the 17th century BC.

One of the most important references of Akkadian literature is the Atrahasis, about the myth of the flood. And from Babylonian literature, the poem Enûma Elish, about the creation of the world.

Artist's interpretation of what the Hanging Gardens of Babylon would look like.

Architecture

Mesopotamia lacked certain materials such as wood, stone and metals, which had to be obtained through trade. One material that was abundant was clay, which favored the manufacture of bricks made of adobe (a mixture of mud and straw). Another material that was found was glass. The architecture was based mainly on the use of bricks with the lintel system, horizontal elements on two supports, and the introduction of the arch and the vault as construction elements.

In this era, ziggurats were developed, Mesopotamian temples in the form of a stepped pyramid. From bottom to top, they consisted of: ramp, vault, dome and terrace. The bases could be rectangular, oval or square in shape. The tombs usually had a corridor and a covered chamber. In this period, the development of palaces became greatly important, with emphasis on gardens and nature. One of the most important references are the hanging gardens of Babylon, one of the seven wonders of the ancient world.

Sculpture

In general, Mesopotamian sculpture was characterized by robust shapes, especially the human figures, which appeared stocky and muscular, with broad backs, protruding cheekbones, wide-open eyes, bushy eyebrows and scarce folds in their clothing, which normally had large stripes.
Relief carvings were made with religious, hunting or military scenes. There are human and animal figures based on real or mythological forms. Human figures had heads that were too large and disproportionate. Mesopotamia developed the so-called conceptual realism where shapes were simplified and regularized according to the law of frontality, i.e., the right and left sides were absolutely symmetrical, and the law of geometry where figures seemed to be enclosed in a cylindrical or cone shape.

THE SCULPTURES AND RELIEFS OF THE ANIMALS WERE VERY REALISTIC IN CONTRAST TO THOSE REPRESENTING HUMAN BEINGS.

Sumerians developed small statues with angular shapes representing the human being with hands on the chest, without hair and colored stones as if they were the eyes. One of the most intriguing aspects of these statues was the use of colored stones for the eyes. The Sumerians skillfully embedded these precious stones within the sculpted faces, imbuing the statues with an enigmatic and lifelike quality. This technique allowed the statues to evoke a sense of vitality and presence, as if the eyes were endowed with a spiritual essence that connected the material world with the realms of the divine.
Arcadians, on the contrary, added the representation of hair and long beard to their figures. For example, the stele of Naram-Sin.
Amorites made very characteristic sculptures of King Gudea of Lagash, with robe and turban and hands, as it was tradition, on his chest.
Babylonians made the famous stele of Hammurabi.
Assyrians made anthropomorphic figures of bulls or winged genies, which flanked the doors of the palaces. On the walls of the palaces, friezes were found with bas-reliefs depicting war scenes (battles), daily scenes or hunting, as, for example, the black Obelisk of Shalmaneser III.

Painting

Painting did not have as many representatives as sculpture, but among the examples that have been found, the law of frontality stands out, where the human figures were represented in profile and with the eye facing forward, although the shoulders and chest kept the natural position. We can also find the hierarchical perspective where the size of the figures was made according to their greater or lesser importance, not according to the greater or lesser distance.

Sculpture of Prince Gudea (2120 a. C.).

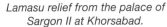

Lamasu relief from the palace of Sargon II at Khorsabad.

Ancient Egypt

Example of Egyptian hieroglyphs.

View of the Book of the Dead, chapters of Padimin written on linen, mummy wrappings. Akhmim, Egypt. Late Period, 664 BC.

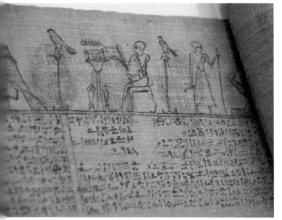

The ancient civilization of Egypt developed along the middle and lower reaches of the Nile River, Upper Egypt to the south and Lower Egypt to the north. Ancient Egypt developed for more than 3000 years, from around 3150 BC until 31 BC when ancient Egypt disappeared as a state and was conquered by the Roman Empire, marking the end of the independent development of its culture.

Art in ancient Egypt flourished with painting and sculpture which were highly symbolic. Egyptian styles were conservative and changed little over the millennia.

The greatest amount of art that has survived time comes from tombs and monuments, making obvious the emphasis they had on the afterlife.

TOMB WALL ART WAS NEVER MEANT TO BE SEEN BY HUMANS AS IT WAS INTENDED FOR THE AFTERLIFE WHEN NECESSARY.

Ancient Egyptian art is a representation of their socioeconomic status and belief system.

Ancient Egyptian art portrayed an idealized view of the world, not a realistic one. There was no tradition of individual artistic expression, as the art had a broader, cosmic purpose.

Writing

Egyptian writing is known as hieroglyphics because the words are not represented with a phonetic sign, but the meaning of these is given with a symbol. The word hieroglyphic comes from Greek and means sacred writing. For the Egyptians, hieroglyphs were the words of the gods and were believed to be their creation.

Illustration from the Book of the Dead, chapter of Hunefer showing the judgment of the dead in the presence of Osiris.

Hieroglyphic symbols were figurative, i.e. they represented recognizable things such as animals or parts of the body. The term "hieroglyphics" comes from the Greek words "hieros," meaning sacred or divine, and "glyphein," meaning to carve or engrave.

According to some theorists, the concept of the written word was first developed in Mesopotamia and reached Egypt through trade. While there was certainly a cross-cultural exchange between the two regions, hieroglyphs are entirely Egyptian in origin.

The ancient Egyptian writing system consisted of 3 basic types of signs: logograms, representing words; phonograms, representing sounds; and determiners, placed at the end of a word to help clarify its meaning. As a result, the number of signs used by the Egyptians reached a thousand hieroglyphs, initially, then reduced to 750 in the Middle Empire period (2,055-1,650 B.C.). Papyrus was the primary portable writing medium in Egypt. It appeared during the first dynasty (3,000-2,890 B.C.) and the earliest known example comes from a blank scroll found in the Tomb of Hemaka, an official of King Den.

The world famous "Book of the Dead" was written with the intention of being a travel guide for the dead to transcend. In it, the heart of the deceased was supposed to be placed on a scale and compared with the weight of a feather. During this trial, several questions were asked to the deceased to know his goodness and likewise, he had to declare 42 negative confessions, for example, "I have not made anyone cry".

Sample of an Egyptian funerary painting clearly showing Anubis and hieroglyphs in the background.

Fresco of Queen Nefertiti (Akhnaton's wife) in her tomb.

Painting

Although Egyptian art is admired worldwide, it has been criticized for being unrefined. Scientists claim that the Egyptians never seemed to have mastered perspective, as there is no interplay of light and shadow in their compositions, they are always two-dimensional, and the figures lack emotion.

The pigments used were mostly minerals chosen to prevent them from falling off over time. It is believed that the binding medium for the paint and the substrate was resin or egg yolk, although this has not been confirmed. Another factor that has helped to preserve the paintings in the tombs and temples has been the extremely dry climate in Egypt.

THE PURPOSE OF SUCH A LEVEL OF PRESERVATION IN PAINTING, IN MOST CASES, WAS TO MAKE A FUTURE LIFE PLEASANT FOR THE DECEASED.

The themes included the journey of the deceased through the afterlife or protective deities presenting the deceased to the gods of the underworld (such as Osiris). Some tomb paintings show activities in which the deceased were involved when they were alive and wished to continue to do so throughout eternity.

The anatomy of the Egyptian paintings was not entirely correct, they wanted to show a profile view and a front view at the same time on the

Relief of the Egyptian god Thoth, behind a seated statue of Ramses II (1,279-1,213 BC), Luxor.

body of humans and animals. Generally, the torso was presented from the front while the limbs and head were shown in profile.

Egyptian painting did not develop a sense of depth, and landscapes are not seen with a visual perspective, but figures vary in size according to their importance rather than their location, yet some paintings depicting hunting and fishing scenes may have vivid water backgrounds in the foreground.

Throughout history, many artists of later times are known, but those of Egypt are completely anonymous. The reason is that their art was functional and created for a practical purpose, while later art was intended for aesthetic pleasure. Functional art is work made for hire, belonging to the individual who commissioned it, in these cases the pharaohs or people in power, while art created for pleasure, even if commissioned, allows for greater expression of the artist's vision and recognition of the author as an individual artist.

Painting is found in murals and in drawings made on papyrus where it can be clearly noticed that the colors had great symbolism. The colors they mainly used were red, blue, green, gold, black and yellow. Blue represented fertility, green for vegetation and rejuvenation, violet for funerary clothing, black for royal figures and death, and gold for divinity.

Along with painting, relief painting was developed. Egyptians used the technique of sunken relief, which is best seen in sunlight so that the contours and shapes are highlighted by the shadows.

Sculpture

In the realm of ancient Egyptian art, full body sculptures hold a prominent place, characterized by a notable and distinctive feature—the positioning of the feet. One of the most significant aspects of these sculptures is the placement of one foot slightly ahead of the other. This particular posture, known as the "Egyptian stance" or "composite pose," was a deliberate artistic choice that served multiple purposes.

The positioning of the feet in this manner was not merely an aesthetic preference but also had practical considerations. It played a crucial role in maintaining the stability and balance of the sculpture. By having one foot placed further forward, the weight distribution was optimized, ensuring that the sculpture would remain steady and upright. This careful attention to balance was essential, especially for freestanding sculptures that needed to withstand the test of time and remain intact. Although seated statues were particularly common as well.

Early period tombs also contained small models of slaves, animals, buildings and objects such as boats, which were necessary for the deceased to continue their lifestyle in the afterlife. Sculptures of small figures of deities, or their animal personifications, were very common, and were made in common materials such as pottery. They also made a large number of small carved objects, from figures of gods to toys and tools.

Bust of Queen Nefertiti.

ALABASTER WAS OFTEN USED FOR EXPENSIVE VERSIONS OF THESE; PAINTED WOOD WAS THE MOST COMMON AND NORMAL MATERIAL FOR SMALL SIZES.

When elaborating statues of their deities, the Egyptians followed very strict conventions, for example, the god of the sky (Horus) was represented

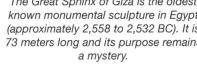

with a falcon's head and the god of funeral rites (Anubis) was always shown with a jackal's head. These conventions were intended to convey the timeless quality of the figures, which for 3,000 years were only slightly altered in their realization.

Architecture

The best examples of Egyptian architecture are the pyramids and temples. The materials used by ancient Egyptian architects to make the sun-dried and kiln-dried bricks were fine sandstone, limestone and granite. They carefully planned all their work. The stones had to fit together precisely, as there was no mortar.

Pyramids are the most predominant examples of architecture in ancient Egyptian culture. Although other civilizations, such as the Maya or the Chinese, also developed pyramids in their architecture, at present, the most enigmatic, deeply studied and fantastic are those of Egypt.

The Great Sphinx of Giza is the oldest known monumental sculpture in Egypt (approximately 2,558 to 2,532 BC). It is 73 meters long and its purpose remains a mystery.

THE PYRAMIDS OF GIZA HAVE STOOD AS IMPRESSIVE MONUMENTS FOR THOUSANDS OF YEARS AFTER THEY WERE BUILT THANKS TO THE EXTENSIVE ARCHITECTURAL KNOWLEDGE OF THE EGYPTIAN PEOPLE.

Although the skill required to build them was accumulated over many centuries before they were erected, today it is a mystery what skill level they developed to build such monuments, as it is believed that at that time there was not enough technology to carry them out.

What is considered to be the first pyramid made by the Egyptians, the step pyramid of Djoser at Saqqara, was made at the end of the Early Dynastic Period. Comparing this monument and its surrounding complex with the tombs in stone block constructions of previous centuries shows how far the Egyptians had advanced in their understanding of architecture, design and construction.

As their search for new architectural forms progressed, the Egyptians abandoned the pyramids and focused on temples. Although today, these temples are only extinct ruins, they inspire as much awe as the pyramids because they expose the Egyptians' fascination with detail, aesthetic beauty and practical functionality that made them architectural masterpieces. These structures still resonate today because they were conceived, designed and built to tell a timeless story that seems familiar to all who visit Egypt today.

Despite their grandeur, the pyramids do not represent the pinnacle of Egyptian architecture, they are only the earliest expression of the culture that would create such magnificent dwellings, monuments and temples.

The construction of temples, although at a modest level, had already familiarized the Egyptians with stone. To better preserve their monuments, they worked stone much more than dry clay.

According to studies, there is no evidence that Hebrew slaves, or any other type, performed work in the construction of the pyramids at Giza, the city of Per-Ramesses, or any other important site in Egypt as popularly depicted in fiction or in the biblical Book of Exodus.

Temple of Amun, Karnak.

America, Africa and Asia

America

Around the 7th millennium BC, the first hunter-gatherer societies emerged in the highlands of Mexico. These societies were dominated by the priestly caste and had great knowledge of mathematics and astronomy. The first artistic findings date back to 1,300 B.C., where clay statuettes of great vivacity were found in Xochipala.

The first American civilization to have great development was the Olmec. They were located in the provinces of Veracruz and Tabasco and their stone sculptures, made with great naturalism, stand out.

Some of the most important references are: The Wrestler, found in Santa María Uxpanapán, and the colossal monolithic heads of up to 3.5 meters high.

In North America, the so-called Oasis American civilizations developed: Hohokam, Mogollon and Anasazi. Archaeological cultural areas that left several monumental remains have also been found that demonstrate a knowledge of ceramics, weaving and irrigation, as well as a fascination with solar movements.

In Peru, the religious complex of Chavín de Huántar (900 B.C.) is a U-shaped structure built as a plaza with sculpted figures of mythological animals and jaguar heads embedded in the walls. Many of these temples were built even before the invention of ceramics in the 3rd millennium BC.

IN THIS REGION OF PERU, THE TEXTILE INDUSTRY, CONSIDERED THE FIRST IN THE WORLD, DEVELOPED NOTABLY, WHERE WEAVINGS MADE WITH LOOMS WITH UP TO 200 THREADS OF DIFFERENT COLORS WERE FOUND.

The complexity and sophistication of the Peruvian textiles were a result of the advanced weaving techniques employed by the skilled artisans. They would meticulously interweave various threads to form intricate patterns, often incorporating symbolic elements and representations of the natural world. These textiles were not only visually stunning but also carried deep cultural and religious significance, reflecting the beliefs, customs, and social structure of the ancient Peruvian societies.

Different cultures developed in Colombia, one of the most important is San Agustín, which by the seventh century B.C. already had a considerable development, and where several hundred monolithic sculptures have been found. Unfortunately, their houses were built with perishable materials, so there are no remains of these, only the holes where they raised the timbers that formed the walls.

Head nailed to a wall in Chavín de Huántar in Peru.

Statues of the Nok civilization in Africa.

Africa

The first culture of great relevance was the Nok, 1st millennium B.C., located in the north of present-day Nigeria. Their most representative art is the terracotta sculptures of human or animal figures (elephants, monkeys, snakes). They sculpted their figures with different hairstyles, sometimes with necklaces and bracelets. The typical canon in Africa was a large head, straight trunk and short limbs.

Generally, the figures were of a religious-magical nature and were used in ceremonies or rites according to their beliefs. In smaller quantities, works of an ornamental nature were made.

In addition to sculpture, they also produced ceramics, jewelry and textiles, as well as metallurgical objects, as iron manipulation had been known since the 6th century BC.

The Kerma and Meroe cultures developed in Sudan and made great advances in monumental constructions in clay, weapons and ceramics.

Other important civilizations in Africa were the Ghana empire, the Sao civilization and the Nubian/Cush peoples.

Asia

China presented some of the most important advances in all of Asia. The stages of artistic development were marked by their reigning dynasties, although their evolution was more uniform than in the West.

UNLIKE THE WEST, THE ARTS WERE EQUALLY VALUED IN CHINA, AS THEY WERE FULLY INTEGRATED INTO ITS PHILOSOPHY AND CULTURE. RELIGION WAS OF GREAT IMPORTANCE IN ARTISTIC EXPRESSION.

The invention of the Chinese script remains a mystery, but it is believed that its inventor was the legendary Cang Jie, who invented the characters as an order of Emperor Huang Di, from 2698 to 2598 B.C., inspired by the traces left by birds.

Chinese literature began with religious works and expounding philosophical ideas between the 10th and 5th centuries BC.

Some of the most important writings developed during the peak of Chinese literature were: The I Ching, a divination manual based on the meaning of eight trigrams, attributed to the mythical emperor Fu Xi; the Shu-king, a ceremonial chronicle; and the Shi King, a classic of poetry.

During the Shang dynasty (1,600-1,046 B.C.), expressions of art such as objects and sculptures in bronze (decorated tableware, masks, statues) were popular. Archaeological excavations in tombs in the Henan area found rich trousseaus of weapons, jewelry and various utensils in bronze, jade and ivory.

During the Zhou dynasty (1,045-256 B.C.), art evolved into stylized and dynamic figures and important works in copper. In this period, agriculture and metallurgy flourished, and Taoism and Confucianism appeared, which would greatly influence art.

During the Qin dynasty (221-206 B.C.) the Great Wall of China was built, which is 2,400 kilometers long and an average of 9 meters high in order to prevent invasions.

Also dating from this date is the Xian Terracotta Army found inside the Mausoleum of Qin Shi Huang (first emperor of unified China). The army has more than 8,000 life-size figures of warriors, chariots and horses. Their anatomy has great precision and naturalism.

In Japan, during the Mesolithic and Neolithic periods (5,000-2,000 B.C.) it remained isolated, so its artistic production is autochthonous.

One of the most important representatives is the Jōmon pottery, the oldest pottery produced by humans, handmade and decorated with rope incisions. As a result of relations with China and Korea since the 1st century BC, large tombs decorated with terracotta cylinders stand out.

View of the Mausoleum of Qin Shi Huang and close-up of some warriors of the Terracotta Army in China.

Dogu statuette from the late Jomon period in Japan.

Ancient Greece

Ancient Rome

Classical art

Classical art marked a significant turning point in the development of human expression, placing a newfound emphasis on society. It flourished in ancient Greece and Rome, where significant scientific and material advancements took place. The finest artistic expressions of this era can be found in painting, sculpture, and architecture, characterized by elegant and refined craftsmanship that reflected the pursuit of physical perfection.

The aesthetics of classical art made valuable contributions to history, showcasing a style rooted in nature and the human form. Harmony and balance prevailed as guiding principles, resulting in rational shapes and volumes. These artistic foundations laid the groundwork for Western art as we know it today.

From this period onward, the recurrence of classical forms became inevitable and integral to the Western artistic tradition. While Roman art developed later, Greek sculpture, pottery, and painting are generally recognized as superior. Greek architecture, too, served as the basis for Roman architectural styles, leaving a lasting legacy in the field.

Ancient Greece

The Parthenon is a Doric temple 69.5 meters long by 30.9 meters wide. Its columns are 10.4 meters high.

Like all other civilizations, the Greeks also learned from the past, adopting the best ideas they encountered when interacting with other cultures and developing their own innovative concepts.

Ancient Greece is often acknowledged for establishing the foundation upon which all Western cultures were built. This remarkable distinction is attributed to their groundbreaking contributions across a wide range of domains, including sports, medicine, architecture, and democracy.

The Greeks made significant contributions and inventions that continue to impact society. These include the development of columns, stadiums, intricate anatomical representations in human sculpture, the establishment of democracy, the jury system, mechanical devices, mathematical reasoning, geometry, advancements in medicine, the inception of the Olympic Games, profound philosophical insights, breakthroughs in astronomy and science, as well as the evolution of theater.

By assimilating knowledge from various sources and fostering their own creative ideas, the Greeks played a pivotal role in shaping the trajectory of Western civilization. Their intellectual and cultural achievements remain influential to this day, leaving an indelible mark on fields ranging from governance and architecture to science and the arts.

GREEK ART DEVELOPED IN THE ARCHAIC (800-496 BC), CLASSICAL (496-336 BC) AND HELLENISTIC (336-146 BC) PERIODS.

It was characterized by looking natural and following the right proportions and measurements. He was inspired by nature and was the starting point of European art.

Architecture

Temples are marvels of Greek architecture, with columns being one of their most notable features. The construction of columns followed different orders, namely Doric, Ionic, and Corinthian. Later, influenced by early Roman architecture, two additional orders emerged: Tuscan and Composite. An order, in essence, comprises a specific style of column, with or without a base, and an entablature.

The Doric column, characterized by its simplicity, rested directly on the stylobate, a stone platform. It featured a vertical fluted shaft, thinner towards the top, and lacked a base. Below a square abacus, a plain capital adorned the column. The Ionic order emerged during the mid-6th century BC. It introduced a base and a volute, or scroll-like, capital. The Ionic column was relatively slimmer and more straightforward compared to the Doric style. It was often accompanied by sculptures carved with circular shapes. The Corinthian order emerged in the 5th century BC and is similar to the Ionic order, but it is crowned with a more ornate capital

Doric order.

Ionic order.

Iori *Corinthian order.* inthus leaves and ferns.

One of the most significant architectural landmarks in the form of a temple in Greece is the Parthenon, completed in 432 BC. It was built to house the statue of Athena and to showcase the glory of Athens to the world.

Other notable examples include the Temple of Zeus in Olympia (460 BC), the Temple of Artemis in Ephesus (430 BC), considered one of the wonders of the ancient world, and the Temple of Poseidon in Sounion (444-440 BC).

Among the most notable architectural inventions of ancient Greece that still resonate in present-day society are the combined stoa, which provided shelter for passersby, the gymnasium with bathing facilities and training grounds, the semicircular theater with ascending rows of seats, and the rectangular stadium for sports.

Ruins of the Theater at the Sanctuary of Apollo at Delphi.

GREEK TEMPLES WERE DESIGNED NOT ONLY TO HOUSE A DEITY'S STATUE BUT ALSO TO BE ADMIRED FROM A DISTANCE. ARCHITECTS EMPLOYED CLEVER OPTICAL TRICKS TO CREATE THE ILLUSION THAT THE STRUCTURE APPEARED PERFECTLY STRAIGHT AND HARMONIOUS WHEN VIEWED FROM AFAR.

The predominant material in public buildings was marble. Although initially the Greeks constructed their structures with wood, gradually they made them more durable by using stone.

Greek temples followed a very similar plan, and most of them were rectangular and peripheral in design, meaning their exterior sides and facades consisted of rows of columns.

Similarly, Greek theaters showcased significant scientific advancements, as their form (an open-air, approximately semicircular arrangement of ascending rows of seats) improved acoustics and are believed to have been used for gatherings during festivals, often featuring theatrical performances, poetry recitals, and music presentations.

Kuros, statue of the Archaic period.

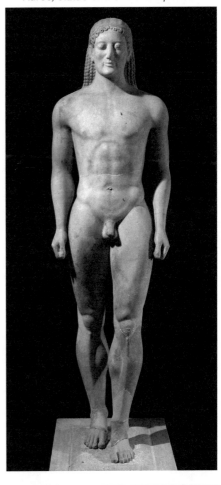

Sculpture

The sculpture of ancient Greece from 800 to 300 BC was initially inspired by Egyptian and Near Eastern art, where the human figure was portrayed in a simple and rather static position. As a result, the depicted individuals often appeared as lifeless as the stone from which they were made. Over the centuries, sculpture evolved into a vision of unique artistic form, adding dynamism to the figures.

Later, Greek artists reached a pinnacle of artistic excellence that captured the human form in a way never seen before and greatly imitated. Greek sculptors were particularly concerned with proportion, balance, and the idealized perfection of the human body. The stone and bronze figures they created have become some of the most recognized works of art ever produced by any civilization.

During the Archaic period of art, the posture of human figures in sculpture became slightly more relaxed, with slightly bent elbows suggesting both tension and movement. In this era, the anatomical features of sculptures became more precise, and the face appeared to have a more accurately depicted smile, with cheeks and noses portrayed with greater detail. During the Archaic period, Kouroi sculptures were popular, representing young men with one foot placed in front of the other, reminiscent of the Egyptian sculpture's pose.

Discobolus, sculpture from the Classic period whose original in bronze, by the Greek sculptor Myron from 450-460 BC. C has been lost. This is a Roman marble copy.

At the beginning of the Classical period, sculptures already depicted a more relaxed and natural posture, even with a bent knee. The muscles and bones appeared lifelike, and the ribcages seemed expanded as if breathing. The position of the sculptures' spinal columns was represented as an S shape, offering movement and balance. The face appeared expressionless, and the smile of the Archaic period disappeared.

The artistic development of Greek sculpture showcases a remarkable evolution, from rigid and static figures to dynamic and natural representations of the human form. These sculptures continue to be celebrated as masterpieces of art and hold significant cultural and historical value.

DURING THE CLASSICAL PERIOD, THE STATUES BREAK AWAY FROM ALL CONVENTION AND BECOME SENSUAL FIGURES THAT SEEM TO JUMP FROM THE PEDESTAL.

Greek sculpture and art, in general, began to focus on proportion, balance, and the perfection of the body. This approach to sculpting was continued by the Romans and continued to influence art in the Renaissance and subsequent periods.

In Greece, during the Classical period, significant advancements were made in medicine, which increased interest in the human body. Thanks to the Olympic Games, athletic bodies were admired, and athletes were considered heroes. The new inspiration for art became sports and aesthetic beauty.

The Classical period was characterized by the pursuit of perfection. Sculptures displayed movement but not emotions on their faces. The body became an independent entity, and anatomical details were prominent, with visible veins, precise ribs, and intercostal muscles. Fabrics were carved with great realism, as if affected by gravity or moved by the wind.

In the transition from the Classical to the Hellenistic period, sculpture artists had already mastered anatomical features and were concerned with line and contrast to create an impression. They explored new techniques and showcased their skills. The art of sculpture in ancient Greece represents a remarkable dedication to capturing the beauty and physicality of the human form, leaving a lasting legacy that influenced artistic movements throughout history. In the Hellenistic era, anatomy meets emotion. The faces of sculptures seem to scream, cry, or suffer. New scenarios are explored, and sculptures of children or scenes from daily life are created. The ideal of beauty is no longer as strict, but emotions and anatomy are exaggerated.

Ceramics were another important form of artistic expression in Greek culture. They were influenced by the Homeric poems.

The preferred materials in Greek sculpture were marble and bronze. Unfortunately, bronze was always in demand for reuse in later periods, while broken

Laocoon and his sons, sculpture from the Hellenistic period (believed to have been made between the 1st century BC or the year 27). Its sculptors were Agesandro, Polidoro and Atenodoro de Rodas.

marble is not very useful, so marble sculpture has survived better for posterity.

Painting and pottery

Unfortunately, due to the passage of time, many examples of Greek painting have been lost. Some of the most important artists were Zeuxis, Parrhasius, and Apelles, but no works by them have survived.
Some of the main examples of painting are found in decorated ceramics, mosaics, and painted clay plaques.
Painters often worked in collective workshops, usually under the supervision of a pottery "master," suggesting that form (sculpture) was actually more important than decoration for the Greeks. Although artists were free to express their art as they wished and were not subject to centralized political control or restrictions, they were undoubtedly influenced by the market demand for particular styles, themes, and fashions.

MANY ARTISTS WERE PROLIFIC IN THEIR PRODUCTION. IN SOME CASES, MORE THAN 200 VASES CAN BE ATTRIBUTED TO THE SAME ARTIST.

Greek potters produced items for practical, everyday use, which served to hold wine, water, oil, and perfumes. Once the optimal practical form of a ceramic had evolved, it was copied and maintained. However, despite this restriction in form, Greek potters and painters were able to express their versatility in the decoration of the vase.
The most common forms of pottery in ancient Greece were: the enócoe for storing wine, the cílica, a ceramic with a wide plate-like shape and horizontal handles, especially practical when lifted from the ground, the hydria, a vase with three handles for holding water, the esquifos or deep bowls, and the lécythos for containing oils and perfumes, usually used in a funerary context.
Some of the decoration styles of the ceramics included:
 ❋ Proto-geometric pottery.
 ❋ Geometric pottery.
 ❋ Black figure pottery.
 ❋ Red figure pottery.
Some cities and regions were consistently eccentric in their decoration, for example, Laconia-Sparta, Cyprus, Crete, and Boeotia, and they preferred to follow their own artistic path rather than imitate the styles of the more dominant populations, such as Athens and Corinth. The most popular proto-geometric designs were precisely painted circles, semicircles, and horizontal lines in black. Large areas of the vase were also painted in black. The geometric style favored a rectangular shape in the main body of the vase. Linear designs (perhaps influenced by contemporary basketry and weaving styles) appeared in this space with a vertical line of decoration on each side. Over time, the geometric style began to include stylized human figures in black. The black-figure style exhibited slender, graceful, and balanced forms. They were depicted in moments prior to actual movement or in repose after exertion. However, not all figures were painted in black. Certain color conventions were adopted, such as white for female flesh and purple-red for clothing and accessories. The black-figure technique was eventually replaced by the red-figure technique, which painted the outlines with a black background.

Two Enochoe or red wine jars.
Approximately 320-300 B.C.

Ceramic with decoration on Hercules attacking a centaur.

Ancient Rome

Despite the great abundance that prevailed in Greece and the advancements in all aspects, Rome conquered its territories in the Macedonian Wars, definitively eliminating the republics and leaving it as the Roman province of Macedonia (146 BC). The Roman Empire is considered to have begun in 27 BC.

Rome reached its greatest extent in 117 AD during the reign of Trajan. It spanned from the Atlantic Ocean in the west to the shores of the Caspian Sea and the Persian Gulf in the east, and from the Sahara Desert in the south to the banks of the Rhine and Danube rivers and the border with Caledonia in the north. It covered approximately 6.5 million square kilometers.

The Romans controlled a vast empire for a long period of time, which led to a great variety and diversity in art, incorporating artistic trends from all corners of the empire, both past and present. The promotion of art reached such a point that it was widely produced and more available than ever before.

THE APPRECIATION OF ROMAN ART BEGAN TO DECLINE DURING THE RENAISSANCE WHEN IT WAS DISCOVERED THAT ROMAN PIECES WERE ACTUALLY COPIES OR AT LEAST INSPIRED BY LOST GREEK ORIGINALS. AS A RESULT, SOME CRITICS EVEN ARGUED THAT "ROMAN" ART DID NOT EXIST.

Thanks to later archaeological excavations, it has been found that Roman art did indeed make significant contributions to Western art in general.

Inheriting the Hellenistic world forged by the conquests of Alexander the Great, the Romans produced art in a wide range of forms: seals, jewelry, glassware, mosaics, ceramics, frescoes, statues, monumental architecture, as well as epigraphy and coins, which were used to embellish the Roman world and convey the significance of their military prowess.

Augustus of Prima Porta. Sculpture from the 1st century built in white marble.

Sculpture

Roman sculpture combined the idealized perfection of earlier classical Greek sculpture with a greater aspiration for realism.

The materials preferred by the Romans above all were bronze and marble. However, since metal has always been in high demand for reuse, most surviving examples of Roman sculpture are in marble.

Reliefs were used to decorate architecture and generally had a political intention.

In Rome, there was a school specifically dedicated to copying Greek originals, especially those from Athens and Rome itself. Roman sculptors also produced miniature copies of Greek originals, often in bronze, which were collected by art lovers and displayed in cabinets in their homes.

By the mid-1st century AD, Roman artists sought to capture and create optical effects of

Relief with a scene from Augustan Ara Pacis. 13 a.m. C. Greco-Roman style.

light and shadow for greater realism, moving away from their Etruscan and Greek roots.

The Romans' urgency to create realistic sculptures may be due, perhaps, to the tradition of keeping wax death masks of deceased family members as close to reality as possible.

BUSTS THAT PORTRAYED THE APPEARANCE OF THE PERSON THEY WERE INSPIRED BY WERE ALSO POPULAR. THE SKIN COULD LOOK OLD, WRINKLED, SCARRED, OR LOOSE, CONTRARY TO THE IDEAL OF PERFECT BEAUTY IN GREEK ART.

During this time, sculpture also became more monumental with enormous statues of emperors, gods, and heroes. One of the most relevant examples is the large bronze statue of Marcus Aurelius on horseback, located in the Capitoline Museums in Rome.

Towards the end of the empire, due to the influence of Oriental art, sculptures tended to lose proportion, with elongated heads and figures that more frequently presented themselves as flat and frontal.

Architecture

It was characterized by its utilitarian and practical nature. The Romans were great engineers and planners. They stood out for their civil architecture, constructing roads, bridges, aqueducts, urban structures, temples, palaces, theaters, amphitheaters, circuses, and triumphal arches.

The Romans transitioned from a trabeated construction style, mainly based on columns and lintels, to one based on solid walls accompanied by arches, and later domes, which were greatly developed by the Romans.

The Romans added the arch to the Greek lintels supported by columns, making it a significant element in Roman architecture. They also developed vaults and domes using ashlar masonry, bricks, and rubble. The Roman Pantheon had the largest dome in the world for over a millennium. It remains the largest unreinforced solid concrete dome to this day.

The Romans pioneered the use of concrete, which marked a departure from traditional forms and materials that allowed limited exploration, such as stone and brick.

Colosseum, Rome, Italy. The classical commands are used, but purely for aesthetic effect.

In column design, the Romans adopted the Greek orders and added the Tuscan order, characterized by a smooth shaft, a capital with a necking and echinus topped with a square abacus. They also introduced the Composite order, a highly decorated style with floral motifs or leaves, seemingly a blend of the Ionic and Corinthian orders.

The period from approximately 40 BC to 230 AD witnessed most of the major achievements of Roman architecture, before the crisis of the third century, where later problems diminished the wealth and organizing power of the central government.

Some of the main references of Roman architecture are: the Colosseum, the Pantheon

of Agrippa, the Theater of Mérida, the Maison Carrée in Nîmes, the Baths of Caracalla, the Aqueduct of Segovia, the Arch of Constantine, and the Tower of Hercules.

Ancient roman aqueduct, Pont du gard, south of France.

Mural Painting

The interiors of Roman buildings and structures of all kinds were lavishly decorated with vibrant and colorful designs.

Mural paintings, frescoes, and stucco were used to create relief effects and were commonly employed in the 1st century BC in public buildings, private houses, temples, tombs, and even military structures throughout the Roman Empire.

THE DESIGNS RANGED FROM COMPLEX REALISTIC DETAILS TO HIGHLY IMPRESSIONISTIC REPRESENTATIONS THAT OFTEN COVERED THE ENTIRE AVAILABLE WALL SPACE, INCLUDING THE CEILING.

The colors used during this period were based on the preferences of those commissioning the murals to the artists, typically earthy and autumnal tones such as darker shades of reds, yellows, and browns. Blue and black pigments were also popular for simpler designs, but evidence from a painting workshop in Pompeii illustrates that a wide range of color shades were available.

Still preserved remains of the House of Livia in Rome.

Themes could include portraits, mythological scenes, trompe-l'oeil architecture (optical illusions with perspective, shading, and other effects), flora, fauna, and even gardens, natural landscapes, and urban settings to create breathtaking 360° panoramas that transported the viewer from the confines of a small room to a limitless world provided by the painter's imagination.

One of the most significant references is the 1st-century BC House of Livia on the Palatine Hill in Rome, which includes a 360° panorama of an impressionist garden. The scene extends across a room, completely disregarding the corners. Another very important example is the 1st-century AD private villa known as the House of the Vettii in Pompeii.

As artistic expression evolved through large-scale individual scenes in mural painting, larger-than-life figures became more common. By the 3rd century AD, one of the best references for mural painting came from the Christian catacombs, where scenes from the Old and New Testaments were depicted.

Mosaic

Roman mosaics were a common feature in both private residences and public buildings throughout the empire, from south to north. Mosaics, also known as opus tessellatum, were compositions made from small squares of marble, tile, glass, ceramics, stone, or shells in black, white, and various colors. Typically, each individual piece measured between 0.5 and 1.5 cm, but fine details, especially in the central panel (emblemata), could be as small as 1 mm.

The designs employed a wide spectrum of colors to complement the surrounding tesserae (mosaic pieces). Opus vermiculatum was a particular type of mosaic that used sophisticated colors and shading to create a painting-like effect. One of the greatest craftsmen of this type of mosaic was Sosus of Pergamon (150-100 BC), whose work, especially his mosaic of drinking doves, was widely copied for centuries.

THE MOSAIC THEMES OFTEN INCLUDED SCENES FROM MYTHOLOGY, GLADIATORIAL CONTESTS, FIGHTS, SPORTS, AGRICULTURE, HUNTING, FOOD, FLORA, AND FAUNA.

They occasionally captured detailed and highly realistic portraits of Romans.

One of the most famous examples of Roman mosaics is found in the House of the Faun in Pompeii, depicting Alexander the Great riding Bucephalus in front of Darius III in his war chariot.

Mosaics not only decorated floors but also vaults (ceilings), columns, and fountains in Roman properties. Roman mosaic artists developed their own styles, and production schools were formed throughout the empire, each cultivating their particular preferences. Large-scale hunting scenes with attempts at perspective were found in the African provinces. Impressionistic vegetation and a close foreground observation were present in the mosaics of Antioch, while in Europe, panels of figures were preferred. The dominant, yet not exclusive, Roman style in Italy used only black and white pieces, a preference that survived until the 3rd century and represented marine scenes, particularly in Roman baths.

Later on, mosaic art that employed two-dimensional and repetitive motifs to create a "carpet" effect would strongly influence Christian churches and Jewish synagogues.

Mosaic of doves from Sosus of Pergamum.

Minor Arts

The minor arts of ancient Rome encompassed a rich array of artistic expressions, representing the Romans' profound appreciation for meticulous craftsmanship and their affinity for working with exquisite materials. These art forms comprised a wide range of objects, each meticulously crafted to showcase the Roman aesthetic sensibility.

Among the diverse range of minor arts, one can find an assortment of jewelry, meticulously designed and adorned with precious gemstones, showcasing the Romans' skill in goldsmithing and lapidary work. These intricate pieces of jewelry included necklaces, bracelets, earrings, rings, and brooches, each crafted with meticulous attention to detail.

Additionally, the Romans excelled in creating small gold portrait busts, capturing the likeness of prominent individuals with remarkable precision and skill. These miniature sculptures served as personal keepsakes or ornamental objects, reflecting the Romans' fascination with portraiture and their desire to immortalize significant figures.

Silver objects were also highly valued in Roman society, reflecting the Romans' refined taste and wealth. Mirrors, cups, plates, and utensils were meticulously crafted from silver, often embellished with intricate engravings and decorative motifs. These objects served both functional and aesthetic purposes, symbolizing the Romans' desire for elegance and luxury in their daily lives.

Roman mosaic of a gypsy girl, 2nd century. Gaziantep Zeugma, Türkiye.

Examples of coins from the Roman Empire.

Paleochristianity
Germanic art
Pre-romanesque art
Byzantine art
Islamic art
Romanesque art
Gothic art
America, Africa, Asia

Medieval art

It is called medieval, or from the Middle Ages, because they were events that occurred in the middle region of the planet (Europe and the Middle East).

Medieval art encompasses the art that developed over a long period in history, from the 5th to the 15th century, spanning Europe, the Middle East, and North Africa. It is considered to have begun with the fall of the Western Roman Empire in 476, although the development of art did not occur as a drastic change but as a gradual evolution.

For a long time, it was considered the Dark Ages because historians and scientists had limited data and information about it, and any thought that contradicted the Church was punished.

Some of the most important events of this period were the fall of the Roman Empire, which occurred after its division due to the invasion of barbarian tribes, the political instability in Constantinople and Ravenna. From this point on, the Church took control, limiting rights and sharing its domains with feudal lords, marking the beginning of the feudal era. During this period, the Crusades took place, movements that aimed to protect Europe from Muslim invasion and forcibly convert people to the religion.

With the establishment of feudalism, the main social groups were the Church, the nobility, and the common people.

Paleochristianity

One of the symbols of Jesus in the paleochristian. You can notice the first and last letters in the Greek of the name of Christ.

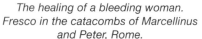

The healing of a bleeding woman. Fresco in the catacombs of Marcellinus and Peter, Rome.

Paleochristian art is also called early Christian art and mainly consists of architecture, painting, and sculpture from the beginning of Christianity until the 6th century. It developed particularly in Italy and the western Mediterranean. It emerged during a period of transition and transformation as the religion gained prominence within the Roman Empire.

Early Christian art in the eastern part of the Roman Empire is generally considered part of Byzantine art, which will be explained later.

The Christian religion was part of a trend in the late Roman Empire filled with mysticism and spirituality.

INITIALLY, CHRISTIANS WERE PERSECUTED AND HUMILIATED, AND THEIR ART REMAINED HIDDEN AS IT WAS CONSIDERED A CULT THAT WAS NOT TOLERATED IN THE EMPIRE.

The first recognizable examples of Christian art consisted of some wall and ceiling paintings from the 2nd century found in the Roman catacombs (underground burial chambers), which continued to be decorated in an incomplete style derived from Roman impressionism until the 4th century. Only in the year 313, Christianity ceased to be persecuted when the Christian emperor Constantine the Great decreed the official tolerance of Christianity. Subsequent imperial patronage brought popularity to the religion, providing it with wealth and many converts from all classes of society. Suddenly, the church needed to produce art and architecture on a more ambitious scale to accommodate and educate its new members and reflect its new social importance.

Influenced by both Roman and Hellenistic traditions, Paleochristian art often conveyed religious themes and symbols, depicting scenes from the Bible, martyrs, saints, and the life of Jesus Christ. The art of this period exhibits a blend of classical elements with distinct Christian symbolism. Different artistic styles developed in different geographical areas.

Painting

The painting of this period had its roots in classical Roman style, which later became a more abstract and simplified artistic expression. The ideal was not physical beauty but spiritual feeling. Human figures became subjects rather than individuals and often had large, fixed eyes, which, according to Christians, were windows to the soul. Symbols were frequently used, and compositions were flat and hieratic to focus on and clearly visualize the main idea.

Thanks to the catacombs, some of the earliest examples of Christian iconography were found, which tended to be symbolic. The scenes depicted were religious and allegorical.

For example, a simple representation of a fish was enough to allude to Christ, and bread and wine invoked the Eucharist.

During the 3rd and 4th centuries, in the catacomb paintings and other manifestations, Christians began to adapt familiar pagan prototypes and give them new meanings. The first figurative representations of Christ, for example, often showed him as the good shepherd by directly borrowing a classical prototype. Other times he was depicted in the form of a god or hero, like Apollo or Orpheus. Only later, when the religion itself had gained certain power, did the representation of Jesus take on more exalted attributes.

The first scenes of Christ's life to be represented were his miracles. The passion, particularly the crucifixion, was generally avoided until the religion was well established.

In architectural painting, church walls were decorated with paintings or mosaics to instruct the faithful.

One of the main references is the Papal Basilica of Santa Maria Maggiore in Rome, which has an extensive program of mosaics depicting scenes from the Old and New Testaments that began in 432. Painting also illustrated liturgical books and other manuscripts. Thanks to painting, miniature and manuscript illumination also developed.

Papal Basilica of Santa Maria Maggiore in Rome.

Architecture

The first manifestations occurred in cemeteries or catacombs, which also served as meeting points for the persecuted.

Later, churches and sanctuaries were built throughout the empire, many sponsored by Constantine himself. These buildings were often basilicas with five naves, such as the Old St. Peter's Basilica in Rome, or basilica-like buildings centered around a round or polygonal sanctuary, such as the Church of the Nativity in Bethlehem. This suggests that the basilica transitioned from having a civil purpose to a religious one.

Basilicas generally consisted of three parts on the interior: an access atrium, the body of the basilica divided into three naves, and the presbytery, where the altar is located.

Some of the main references are St. Peter's Basilica in the Vatican, St. John Lateran, St. Lawrence, and St. Clement in Rome, and St. Apollinaris in Ravenna.

Statuette of the Good Shepherd.

Sculpture

Initially, except for differences in subject matter, Christian and pagan works seemed very similar. In fact, it is possible to demonstrate that the same workshop of artists sometimes produced sculptures for both Christian and non-Christian purposes.

Relief, figurative representation on a sarcophagus.

Large-scale sculpture was not popular, but relief sculpture, which accompanied architecture, was used for sarcophagi, such as the one of Junius Bassus (died in 359), and ivory carvings were widely used.

The reliefs found today from the paleochristian era show that until the 6th century, a defined portrait of Christ had been established. Jesus generally appears with a youthful appearance in everyday life scenes. In images of his glory, he appears older, with a beard and a serious expression.

Germanic Art

Detail of the votive crown of the Visigothic king Recesvinto, 672.

The Germanic peoples invaded the Roman Empire, dividing the territory into various kingdoms where the invading peoples became the ruling class. From this moment, new political and cultural entities were created that would solidify throughout the entire Middle Ages, giving rise to the diverse nationalities that exist today.

Germanic art is also referred to as barbarian art. This type of art is usually chronologically centered around the barbarian invasions or the Germanic kingdoms after their Christianization and settlement in the former Roman Empire from the 5th century onwards.

GERMANIC AESTHETICS ARE RECOGNIZABLE AS A CULTURAL CONTRAST TO MEDITERRANEAN ART AND ARE FOUND IN THE ART OF GERMANY, AUSTRIA, AND NORTHERN EUROPE.

Among the Germanic peoples are the Visigoths, who settled in the Iberian Peninsula. The Visigoths developed their own distinctive style of great importance, with notable examples being the goldsmithing of crowns and crosses found in the treasures of Guarrazar and Torredonjimeno.

Metalwork and Decoration

The artistic mediums employed in Germanic art varied, including metalwork, jewelry, sculpture, manuscript illumination, and architecture. The Germanic peoples excelled in metalworking, creating exquisite objects ranging from everyday items to ceremonial and religious artifacts.

Some distinctive features of the nomadic culture that were incorporated into Germanic art were the production of small transportable objects and a taste for filigree and metalwork.

The barbarian peoples excelled in metalworking, creating objects ranging from everyday items to jewelry, ritual objects, and weapons. Prominent among Germanic metalwork are:

* Bracteates: Usually gold medals worn as ornaments.
* Fibulae: Metal pieces used to fasten and connect garments (buttons were not invented until the Middle Ages).
* Enamels: The technique of enameling (fusing powdered glass onto a substrate) on ceramics.

Thanks to cultural contacts from multiple origins throughout Europe and Asia (including the Near and Far East and the steppe region between Eastern Europe and Central Asia), decorative forms based on the polychrome style (found among the Huns and the Black Sea, reaching the goldsmithing of the Visigoths, Franks, and Lombards in the 7th century) or the animal style were developed.

Visigothic church of San Juan de Baños in the town of Baños de Cerrato, Spain.

Architecture

The early architectural manifestations of Germanic art had little relevance due to the scarcity of materials and the lack of design during construction. Typically, they utilized Roman constructions and materials. The most commonly used elements were the round arch and the vault.

During this period, notable Ostrogothic buildings in Italy included the Mausoleum of Theoderic in Ravenna.

VISIGOTHIC ARCHITECTURE INCORPORATED THE USE OF ASHLAR MASONRY, THE HORSESHOE ARCH, AND VAULTING, WHETHER BARREL OR RIBBED.

Some examples of Visigothic churches include:
* Basilica with three aisles: San Juan de Baños, Palencia.
* Church with a single nave and lateral chambers: San Pedro de la Mata, Toledo.
* Greek cross plan church: Santa Comba de Bande, Ourense.

In Spain, Visigothic architecture included the particular use of the horseshoe arch and, at times, Latin cross plans with churches of varying heights.

Visigoth horseshoe arch in the sanctuary of Santa Eulalia de Bóveda.

Sculpture

The Germanic peoples used stone sculpture for the decoration of churches and baptisteries, creating flat reliefs on capitals and sarcophagi following late Roman models. Some of the main references are the reliefs of Poitiers in France or Cividale in Italy.

Sculptures often depicted biblical figures, saints, and narrative scenes.

The Visigoths incorporated figurative sculpture into churches through frieze reliefs and capitals. Some of the most important references are Quintanilla de las Viñas in Burgos and San Pedro de la Nave in Zamora. Numerous workshops in Italy and Gaul developed ivory carving, which was later adapted for the production of covers for the most exclusive books. Since ivory had little monetary use and was difficult to recycle, these works became original pieces, unlike many works made of precious metals for which no traces remain.

Painting

In Germanic painting, miniatures stood out. Miniature portraits were very popular, as well as scenes from everyday life and landscapes.

Some of the main references for miniatures are the sacramentaries (ancient Catholic books containing prayers, liturgical ceremonies, and administration of the sacraments) from Luxeuil and Gelasianus in the Vatican.

Manuscript illumination, the illustration of religious books through miniatures with included or separate paintings or drawings in scenes or compositions, was developed in painting. Manuscript illumination included various ornamental motifs such as drawings enhancing the capital letters of certain pages, illustrated column dividers representing fictitious architectures, arabesques, stems, and leaves that adorned the margins. Miniature painting and manuscript illumination flourished, producing intricately detailed illustrations in religious texts.

Pages from the Gelasian sacramentary.

Pre-Romanesque art

Interior of the Palatine Chapel in Aachen, the remaining component of Charlemagne's palace. Example of Carolingian architecture.

Pre-Romanesque art refers to the artistic manifestations developed in Europe from the coronation of Charlemagne in the year 800 until around the year 1000. From this point on, Romanesque art became the prevailing style accepted throughout the European continent.

Pre-Romanesque art encompasses different artistic movements that are difficult to precisely define, emerging in the early Christian regions of the Western Roman Empire. This period bridges the gap between Early Christian art and Romanesque art.

The fall of the Western Roman Empire and the barbarian invasions led to political instability and cultural decline. The Dark Ages represent a scarcity of information and discontinuity in sources.

Carolingian Art

The coronation of Charlemagne in the year 800, King of the Franks and later Holy Roman Emperor, sparked a cultural revival known as the Carolingian Renaissance. Charlemagne enacted church reform, and art flourished primarily under the patronage of the court.

CHARLEMAGNE INVITED THE BEST SCHOLARS FROM ALL OVER EUROPE TO HIS COURT TO PROVIDE ADVICE ON POLITICS, THE CHURCH, ART, AND LITERATURE.

Artists worked exclusively for the emperor, members of his court, and the bishops.

The art was based on classical models but infused with Christian themes. Alcuin of York, an English cleric and master of Charlemagne, inspired the Carolingian art movement.

Carolingian architecture aimed to emulate Roman styles, using piers instead of columns with round arches and wooden roofs or barrel vaults.

In painting, there was a suggestion of spatiality and perspective. The figurative art of this period is easily recognizable, as Carolingian artists sought to restore the illusion of the third dimension, using classical drawings as models to create more convincing spatial illusions.

The Carolingians were the first to incorporate musical instruments for compositions, with Gregorian chant prevailing.

Ottonian Art

This art corresponds to the period during the reigns of Otto I, Otto II, and Otto III (approximately between 930 and 980).

Ottonian architecture incorporated elements from the Carolingian style. Some of the most notable examples can be found in San Ciriaco in Genrode, St. Michael's in Hildesheim, and Speyer Cathedral.

The visual arts continued to be influenced by Byzantine styles, with notable examples in bronze sculpture.

Bronze carved doors of Saint Michael of Hildesheim. Sample of Ottonian art.

As illuminated manuscripts were the primary artistic form of the time, Ottonian artists received direct support from the emperor and created remarkable works. Some frescoes can be found in the Church of St. George in Oberzell Monastery.

Celtic Art

This type of art mainly developed in the recently evangelized British Isles. Due to the use of wood in construction, few examples of Celtic architecture remain, although notable mentions include the churches of Deerhurst and Bradford-on-Avon.

THE MOST PROMINENT EXAMPLES OF SCULPTURE ARE THE IRISH CROSSES ADORNED WITH ELABORATE RELIEFS, SUCH AS THOSE IN MOONE, KELLS, AND MONASTERBOICE.

Miniature painting stood out in Celtic art, greatly influenced by the Carolingian style. The most notable references can be found in the Winchester School, to which the illuminated manuscript known as the Pontifical of Saint Æthelwold belongs, created between 975 and 980, including over twenty fully illuminated pages.

Irish high cross example of Celtic sculpture.

Viking Art

Viking architecture was characterized by the use of wood and the construction of pyramid-shaped churches with high, pointed roofs. The projecting sections of the churches exhibited great verticality, and their interiors resembled Viking assembly halls. One of the most representative examples is the Norwegian church of Borgund.
The Vikings were skilled in metalwork, with notable examples being fibulae with long needles and swords adorned with terminal buttons and rings on the hilt.

Borgund Viking Church.

Asturian Art

Pre-Romanesque architecture in Asturias (the first Christian kingdom established on the Iberian Peninsula after the Muslim conquest) spanned from 711 to 910 and stands as the most notable example of art.
In architecture, they used ashlar masonry walls, round arches, barrel vaults with transverse arches, and exterior buttresses. These structures often had a fortress-like appearance, reflecting the defensive nature of the time and the need for protection against invasions. Some of the main references are the Church of San Julián de los Prados, San Miguel de Lillo, Santa Cristina de Lena, and San Salvador de Valdediós.

Hilt of a Viking sword.

Byzantine art

On the left, icon of the archangel Gabriel, 13th century. On the right The Cambrai Madonna, 1340.

Byzantine art includes architecture, painting, and other visual arts produced during the Middle Ages in the Byzantine Empire, centered in Constantinople and other regions under its influence.

The Byzantine Empire was the eastern part of the Roman Empire that survived despite the fall of the western part..

THE PICTORIAL AND ARCHITECTURAL STYLES THAT CHARACTERIZED BYZANTINE ART, FIRST CODIFIED IN THE 6TH CENTURY, PERSISTED WITH REMARKABLE HOMOGENEITY WITHIN THE EMPIRE UNTIL ITS DISSOLUTION WITH THE FALL OF CONSTANTINOPLE TO THE TURKS IN 1453.

Byzantine art was highly influenced by religious ideas, particularly the carefully controlled artistic translation of church theology.

Three distinct stages can be identified in Byzantine art: one from the 6th century (coinciding with the reign of Justinian), another from the 9th century until the capture of Constantinople by the Crusaders in 1204, and the third in the 14th century with the Palaiologan dynasty.

Various elements contributed to the overall cultural and artistic achievements of the Byzantine Empire. Here are some key features that were highly significant during this era:

* Iconography: Byzantine religious art placed great emphasis on iconography, which involved the creation of religious images, especially icons. Icons were considered sacred and were venerated.
* Mosaic Art: Byzantine mosaics were intricate and visually stunning artworks created by assembling small pieces of colored glass, stone.

Hagia Sophia in Turkey, a former Orthodox patriarchal basilica, later converted into a mosque and now a museum.

Architecture

Architecture and painting evolved under the close scrutiny of the church, which controlled artistic affairs, resulting in a uniform and anonymous style. The result was a sophisticated style and an expression of spirituality rarely paralleled in Western art.

Early Byzantine architectural constructions were characterized by the longitudinal basilica. The ecclesiastical plan developed in Italy favored the extensive use of large domes and vaults. Stone and brick were the primary materials used, with exteriors covered in relief-decorated stone plates and interiors adorned with mosaics.

Columns and cubical capitals decorated with reliefs on two planes were widely used. The round arch and the dome on pendentives were also employed. Due to the importance given to the dome, the most common typology was a centrally planned structure with two lateral chambers, an altar under a baldachin, and a choir at the back.

Religion had a hierarchical view of the Universe, which was emphasized through the decoration of

churches with frescoes or, more commonly, mosaics, covering domes, walls, and vaults in a complete fusion of architectural and pictorial expression.

At the top of the central dome, there was often a depiction of God, with angels and archangels beneath. The walls portrayed saints or narrative scenes from the life of Christ. The Virgin Mary was often depicted on a half-dome covering one of the four radial arms, with the congregation below. The entire church thus formed a microcosm of the universe.

Some of the most important references in Byzantine architecture include the Church of Saints Sergius and Bacchus, the Church of Saint Irene, and the Hagia Sophia.

Painting

Mature Byzantine style evolved through the standardization of late classical forms in early Christian art, based on the dynamics of lines and flat areas of color rather than form. Physical features of individuals were suppressed in favor of a standardized facial type, figures were flattened, and draperies reduced to swirling line patterns.

> THE PRIMARY EFFECT OF BYZANTINE PAINTING WAS THE DISAPPEARANCE OF THE INDIVIDUAL HUMAN FIGURE, REPLACED BY A SPIRITUAL PRESENCE WHOSE STRENGTH DEPENDED ON THE VIGOR OF THE LINE AND THE BRILLIANCE OF THE COLOR.

Byzantine painting was both more remote and more immediate than classical naturalism. It can be recognized by the frontal poses and the typical Byzantine depiction with large eyes, penetrating gaze, and the characteristic use of a golden background, giving the impression that the painting is suspended somewhere between the wall and the viewer.

Manuscript illumination, while unable to achieve the impressive effects of monumental painting and mosaic, played a significant role in spreading Byzantine style and iconography throughout Europe.

In the later period of Byzantine painting, the schools of Cyprus, Thessaloniki, Crete, Venice, and Moscow stood out, where painting replaced mosaics, especially in icon painting on wooden panels.

Sculpture

Apart from its own achievements, the importance of Byzantine art for religious art in Europe cannot be overstated. Byzantine art forms spread through trade to Italy and Sicily, where they persisted in modified forms until the 12th century and became influential in shaping Italian Renaissance art. Through the expansion of the Eastern Orthodox Church, Byzantine art also reached Russia.

Small sculptures were produced, with the most common use being small ivory relief carvings used for book covers, reliquary boxes, and similar objects. Stone carvings were also created, featuring images of consecration, depicting Christ with his hands over the heads of emperors.

Other miniature arts such as embroidery, goldsmithing, and enamelwork flourished in the sophisticated and wealthy society of Constantinople.

Interior of the monastery church in Daphne, Greece. Eleventh century. You can see the Byzantine dome mosaic of Christ Pantokrator.

The tree of Jesse, illuminated manuscript. Image: Bibliotheque Municipale de Douai, France— Giraudon/Art Resource, New York.

Islamic art

Lobed arch.   *Mixtilinear arch.*

Half point arch.   *Banked arch.*

Horseshoe arch   *Tumid pointed arch.*

Types of arches most used in Islamic architecture.

Islamism emerged with the Hegira of Muhammad in 622 and became a widely spread religion in North Africa, reaching Europe through the conquest of the Iberian Peninsula and the Balkan region after the fall of the Byzantine Empire.

INITIALLY, ISLAMIC ART EXHIBITED A GREAT SENSE OF UNITY REFLECTED IN THE USE OF CALLIGRAPHY, A COMMON FORM OF WRITING THROUGHOUT THE ISLAMIC WORLD.

Over time, Islam spread among diverse peoples, blending with different cultures and giving rise to numerous manifestations and stylistic variations in art depending on the region.

For most people, the Muslim world during the medieval period (900-1300) is synonymous with the Crusades. Although this period was marked, in part, by military conflicts, it was overwhelmingly an era of peaceful exchanges of goods and ideas between the West and the East.

The main expression of Islamic art was seen in architecture since the church forbade the creation of figurative images, posing a serious obstacle for painting and sculpture. The Seljuk dynasty, which controlled the rest of the empire from 1081 to 1307, was great supporters of education and the arts, founding several important madrasas, or schools, during their reign. The congregational mosques they erected began to incorporate a four-iwan plan, featuring four immense pointed arch-shaped doors (iwans) in the center of each wall surrounding a courtyard.

Architecture

During the early period, the emphasis was placed on the importance of palace architecture. Mosques were commissioned by royalty, and every aspect of their decoration was of the highest caliber, from intricately carved wooden minbars (where the spiritual leader guides the prayers within the mosque) to handmade metal lamps.

Before the 13th century, in what is now Egypt, Syria, Iraq, and Turkey, almost all mosques followed the so-called Arab plan, which included a large courtyard and a hypostyle prayer hall.

Islamic architecture prominently featured the use of pointed arches. Between 711 and 1492, the horseshoe arch was used in the Iberian Peninsula, as a heritage of Visigothic art. The pointed arch was employed in overlapping and intersecting patterns, leading to the emergence of lobed arches, typically with 3 or 5 lobes. The vaults used were either stalactite or ribbed vaults (formed by the intersection of two pointed barrel vaults). Due to the prohibition of creating iconographic images of religious scenes, the art of ornamental decoration in architecture flourished with great significance. Various techniques such as stucco, alabaster, marble, mosaic, or painting were employed, often featuring abstract designs, epigraphic motifs, vegetation, or interlacing patterns. These distinct Islamic decorations are easily identifiable as they appear highly intricate, almost exaggerated in detail. The primary typology of Islamic places of worship was the mosque, which consisted of the following parts:

❋ Courtyard or sahn.
❋ Tower or minaret.

Istanbul Blue Mosque.

* Prayer hall or haram.
* Rear or qibla.
* Chapel or mihrab.
* Arched area or maqsura.

Some of the main references for mosques during this period include the Umayyad Mosque in Damascus, the Dome of the Rock and Al-Aqsa Mosque in Jerusalem, the Great Mosque of Samarra, the Ibn Tulun Mosque in Egypt, the Jameh Mosque of Isfahan, the Timurid Mosque in Samarkand, and the Blue Mosque in Istanbul.

In the area of al-Andalus (the Iberian Peninsula and Septimania region under Muslim rule during the Middle Ages), Islamic architecture flourished during the Emirate of Córdoba (756-929). They inherited Hispano-Roman and Visigothic forms, using the horseshoe arch enclosed in an alfiz, with alternating red and white voussoirs as seen in the Mosque of Córdoba.

Mosque of Cordoba.

During the Mamluk period (1250-1517), where Turkish slaves who served as soldiers for the Ayyubid Sultanate rebelled and rose to power, Cairo became the artistic and economic capital of the Islamic world. The period witnessed a great production of art and architecture, particularly commissioned by the reigning sultans. The Mamluks built countless mosques, madrasas, and mausoleums that were furnished and decorated with exquisitely designed pieces.

Painting

Due to the prohibition (to avoid idolatry) in Islamic art, painting consisted of ornamental decorations with abstract or geometric motifs. Small pictorial expressions took a secondary role in miniatures or frescoes as decorative motifs. In religious temples, painting was reduced to epigraphy.

Rather than focusing on realistic depictions of figures or scenes, Islamic painters excelled in the art of intricate and delicate ornamentation. This emphasis on decorative elements allowed artists to explore the potential of geometric patterns, calligraphy, arabesques, and interlacing designs. These ornamental decorations were meticulously crafted, showcasing the skill and creativity of Islamic artists.

In the Islamic world, calligraphy was considered an art. The suras of the Qur'an were divine words.

Sculpture

Ivory was one of the most commonly used materials for the production of small objects such as luxury boxes or chests. One of the most significant references is the Pyxis of al-Mughira, a true masterpiece adorned with figurative scenes that are difficult to interpret.

During the Mamluk period, decorative objects, particularly glasswork, became famous throughout the Mediterranean. The empire benefited economically and culturally from the trade of these goods, as Mamluk artisans began to incorporate elements obtained through contact with other groups. Trade with China gradually grew, and the Mamluks initiated the production of blue and white ceramics as an imitation of the typical porcelain from the Far East.

Ivory box of Al-Mughira Pyx.

Romanesque art

The Romanesque art refers to the art developed in Western Europe from around the year 1000 until the emergence of the Gothic style in the 12th century. It emerged when Europe first regained a measure of political stability after the fall of the Roman Empire.

The Romanesque style reached its peak between 1075 and 1125 in France, Italy, Great Britain, and the German lands. It encompasses the architecture, sculpture, and painting characteristic of the first of the two great international artistic periods that flourished in Europe during the Middle Ages, with a consolidated identity after the transition from Latin to vernacular languages.

THE TERM "ROMANESQUE" REFERS TO THE FUSION OF ROMAN, CAROLINGIAN, OTTONIAN, BYZANTINE, AND LOCAL GERMANIC CULTURES THAT SHAPED A MATURE STYLE.

Although perhaps the most notable advancements in Romanesque art were made in France, the style became popular throughout Europe, except in areas in the East that retained a full Byzantine tradition. Its geographical distribution gave rise to a wide variety of local types.

Like in previous periods, all Romanesque art was aimed at exalting and disseminating the Christian religion. During this period, literature was predominantly in the hands of the clergy in Latin, although secular writings emerged in the vernacular language.

The art of this period encompasses architecture, sculpture, and painting, representing the first of the two major international artistic epochs that thrived in Medieval Europe, characterized by a transition from Latin to vernacular languages.

Detail of the Royal Portico of the Cathédrale Notre-Dame de Chartres.

Architecture

Romanesque architecture emerged around the year 1000 and evolved into the Gothic style by 1150.

During this period, several large monastic orders appeared, especially the Cistercians, Cluniacs, and Carthusians. These orders expanded rapidly, establishing churches throughout Western Europe. Their churches had to be larger than previous ones to accommodate a greater number of priests, monks, and pilgrims who wished to see the relics of saints kept in the churches. To fulfill this function, Romanesque churches extensively used the semicircular Roman arch for windows, doors, and arcades, barrel vaults, or ribbed vaults to support the roofs with the help of massive pillars and walls to contain the extremely strong outward thrust of the arches. The basic plans of the church that evolved in France became the most commonly used types, expanding on the plan of the early Christian basilica. The typical Romanesque church had side aisles along the nave with galleries

Basilica of Saint Saturnin of Toulouse. Image: Didier Descouens.

above them, a large tower above the crossing of the nave, and smaller towers at the western end of the church. The barrel vaults of Romanesque churches were typically divided by engaged columns and transverse arches into square bays or compartments. This compartmentalization was an essential feature that distinguished Romanesque architecture from its Carolingian and Ottonian predecessors.

Some of the most important architectural references are the Cluny Monastery, Autun Cathedral of Saint Lazarus, Conques Abbey Church of Sainte-Foy, Toulouse Basilica of Saint-Sernin, Périgueux Cathedral of Saint-Front, and Caen Abbey Church of Saint-Étienne in France.

Sculpture

Sculpture was primarily an architectural accompaniment. The art of monumental sculpture was revived in Western Europe after nearly 600 years of absence. Relief sculpture was used to represent scenes from biblical history and church doctrine on the capitals of columns (top part of the column) and around the massive doors of churches.

TO PRODUCE A DISTINCTIVE STYLE OF SCULPTURE, A RELATIVE STYLISTIC FREEDOM WAS COMBINED WITH A HERITAGE OF ANGULAR GERMANIC DESIGN, DRAWING INSPIRATION FROM RELIGION.

Natural objects were freely transformed into visionary images that derived their power from abstract linear design and expressive distortion and stylization.

This spiritualized art revealed the Romanesque concern for transcendent values, in sharp contrast to the markedly more naturalistic and humanistic sculpture of the subsequent Gothic period.

In Spain, one can find some artists who made significant contributions to architectural sculpture. For example, the Catalan workshops of Ripoll and the Pyrenees region, the ivory workshops of León (Crucifix of Ferdinand I), the workshops along the Camino de Santiago, the Facade of Las Platerías of Santiago Cathedral, and the cloister of Silos.

Painting

The majority of painting was mural, covering the interior walls of churches. The surviving fragments show that mural painting imitated the sculptural style. One aspect of Romanesque art that is worth mentioning is the inclusion of narrative cycles in the sculptural and painted decorations of churches. These narrative cycles were visual storytelling devices that depicted biblical stories, the lives of saints, and other religious narratives. The illumination of manuscripts also followed the sculptural trend towards linear stylization in the decoration of initials and margins. The main reference for Romanesque painting is found in the Romanesque church of San Clemente de Tahull.

Both sculpture and painting incorporated a wide range of common new themes such as contemporary theological works, biblical events, and the lives of saints, reflecting the general resurgence of learning.

The Gothic art began to replace Romanesque in the mid-12th century.

Two-headed Janus. Romanesque stone sculpture in high relief, in the Museo del Duomo, Ferrara, Italy. Image: SCALA, Art Resource, New York.

Frescoes in the Church of San Clemente de Tahull, in the Bohí Valley. In the year 2000 it was declared a World Heritage Site by Unesco.

Gothic art

Miniature of Bernardo de Clairvaux from the year 1267.

Gothic corresponds to the second great international era where art flourished in panel painting, stained glass, frescoes, illuminated manuscripts, sculpture, and architecture in Western and Central Europe during the Middle Ages.

Gothic art developed from Romanesque art and lasted from the mid-12th century to the late 15th century, and into the 16th century in some areas, predominantly in France. By the late 14th century, it had evolved into a more secular and natural style that would continue for another century until the Renaissance.

The term "Gothic" was coined by Italian classical writers of the Renaissance, who attributed the non-classical ugliness of medieval architecture or the lack of adherence to Greek classical standards to the barbarian Gothic tribes that had destroyed the Roman Empire and its classical culture in the 5th century.

THE EMERGENCE OF THE GOTHIC STYLE REPRESENTS THE PINNACLE OF ACHIEVEMENTS FOR UNIFIED CHRISTIANITY AND THE TRIUMPH OF THE PAPACY.

It is a successful and inspiring synthesis of religion, philosophy, and art. Ultimately, Gothic art was a representation of the unification of secular and religious ideals.

Amiens Cathedral. 1,266.

Architecture

During the Middle Ages, people lived in one area, afraid to venture far from their lands due to attacks from barbarian and invading groups. Lords offered their lands to the working class in exchange for protection from their knights.

This was known as a kingdom. To protect the kingdoms from each other, large and strong castles were built, which ultimately gave rise to Gothic architecture.

Gothic architecture was characterized by pointed arches, trefoils, quatrefoils, and other architectural ornaments that were also adopted in metalwork such as reliquaries and liturgical vessels, ecclesiastical vestments, and precious diptychs intended for private devotion.

Early Gothic

The birth of architecture in the Early Gothic period is considered to be on June 11, 1144. The Royal Abbey of St. Denis set a precedent with its radiating chapels and glass mosaics that builders would try to imitate for over half a century. Early Gothic architecture refers to the architectural style that emerged in France in the mid-12th century and spread throughout Europe during the 13th century.

The existence of the Gothic style can be attributed to Bernard of Clairvaux and Abbot Suger. The constructions highlighted purity of contour, simplicity, and a form and light particularly conducive to meditation.

High Gothic

Milan Cathedral.

Half a century after the emergence of Gothic architecture, on June 10, 1194, a great fire destroyed the city of Chartres and its cathedral. The only parts of the cathedral that remained were the crypt, the western towers, and the Royal Portal. This newly rebuilt Chartres Cathedral is considered the first of the High Gothic style constructions.

The main characteristic of the High Gothic style is the use of flying buttresses. As a result of using flying buttresses, the need for Romanesque walls was eliminated. The organic and fluid quality of the interior of High Gothic was enhanced by the decompartmentalization of the interior, so that the nave appears as a single continuous volume of space.

Due to the large windows, more light entered the interior of the structure. Light was of great importance to Gothic architects.

Late Gothic

Late Gothic architecture was also known as the "extravagant" style due to the flamboyant appearance of pointed tracery. The style had reached its maturity by the late 15th century.

The Late Gothic period would change the structure of Western Europe.

Sculpture

Gothic sculpture evolved from the early rigid and elongated styles, partly Romanesque, to a spatial and naturalistic sense in the late 12th and early 13th centuries.

THE GOTHS RECOVERED THE INFLUENCES OF ANCIENT GREEK AND ROMAN SCULPTURES THAT WERE PRESERVED AND INCORPORATED INTO THE TREATMENT OF DRAPERY, FACIAL EXPRESSION, AND POSE.

Gothic sculpture was born on the walls of the Basilica of Saint-Denis in the mid-12th century. Before this, there was no tradition of sculpture in the Île-de-France region, so sculptors were brought from Burgundy. These sculptors created revolutionary figures that served as columns in the Western portal of Chartres Cathedral, a completely new invention that would be taken as a model for many generations of sculptors.

During this period, there was an insatiable demand for figurative sculptures to adorn portals, archivolts, tympanums, choir screens, and foliate capitals of cathedrals and churches. Gothic sculpture became regional as sculptors moved to work from one cathedral to another instead of simply staying in one area. An ideal example is that of the sculptors of Reims Cathedral, who later built sculptures at Bamberg Cathedral, about two hundred miles away.

Representation of the Adoration of the Magi, sculptures by Jacques de Landshut in the Notre Dame Cathedral in Strasbourg. 1,494-1,505.

49

Door of the Bamberg cathedral.

The Cathedral of Bamberg in Germany, since 1225, had the largest ensemble of sculptures from the 13th century, culminating in 1240. It housed the first equestrian statue in Western art since the 6th century.

In England, sculpture was mainly limited to tombs and non-figurative decorations, partly attributable to Cistercian iconoclasm.

By the 12th century in Italy, there still existed a classical influence, but the Gothic style managed to make its way in. It gained prominence mainly through pulpit sculptures such as those in the Baptistery of Pisa (1269) and Siena. A late masterpiece of Italian Gothic sculptures is the series of Scaliger tombs in Verona from the early and late 14th century.

The Dutch-Burgundian sculptor Claus Sluter marked the beginning of the end of Gothic sculpture with his preference for naturalism, evolving towards the classical Renaissance style in the late 15th century.

Some of the most influential sculptors of the time were:

* ✳ Mastro Guglielmo.Italian.
* ✳ Benedetto Antelami. 1178-1196. Italian.
* ✳ Nicola Pisano. 1220-1284. Italian.
* ✳ Guido Bigarelli. 1238-1257. Italian.
* ✳ Evrard d'Orleans. 1292-1357. French.
* ✳ Peter Parler. 1330-1399. German.
* ✳ Claus Sluter. 1350-1406. Flemish.
* ✳ Giovanni Bon. 1355-1443. Italian.

Painting and Stained Glass

Gothic painting did not appear until the 13th century, almost 50 years after the emergence of architecture and sculpture.

THE TRANSITION FROM ROMANESQUE TO GOTHIC PAINTING IS VERY IMPRECISE AND DOES NOT HAVE A CLEAR SEPARATION.

Stained glass windows of Santa Capilla in Paris, built in 1248.

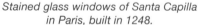

It is believed to have begun when a darker, more emotional style of painting emerged compared to the earlier period. This transition first occurred in England and France around 1200, in Germany in 1220, and in Italy around 1300. Dark themes and strong emotions became increasingly pronounced in late Gothic art.

Painting as the representation of images on a surface was practiced in four main forms in the Gothic period: frescoes, panel paintings, manuscript illumination, and stained glass.

Frescoes were already used in the early Christian and Romanesque periods in southern Europe as the main narrative pictorial art on church walls, so they continued as a tradition.

In the north, stained glass was the chosen art form until the 15th century. The transition from Romanesque to Gothic architecture meant a reduction in walls, spectacularly replaced by stained glass, giving great importance to interior lighting. The use of stained glass led to the search for other mediums to represent religious images, such as panel painting. The impact of stained glass was incomparable. For many, it resembled the light of heaven, a spiritual light that filtered through the soul. The Gothic ambiance seems to be inspired by the Gospel of John, which speaks of light.

Panel paintings began in Italy in the 13th century and rapidly spread throughout Europe, so that by the 15th century, they had become the dominant form of art. Panel painting marked the birth of canvas painting. Oil painting on canvas did not become popular until the 15th and 16th centuries and became a hallmark of Renaissance art.

Illuminated manuscripts were one of the few surviving pieces of Gothic art from the passage of time.

> THIS ERA WAS ONE IN WHICH ARTISTS BEGAN TO ASSIGN THEIR OWN NAMES TO THEIR WORKS, STARTING TO BE RECOGNIZED INDIVIDUALLY.

It is difficult to encapsulate Gothic painting within a single set of characteristics as they depend on the school being discussed. In general, the following characteristics can be pointed out:

* Drawing is of great importance, defining forms, marking models, and creating compositional rhythms, over color.
* At the beginning of the period, backgrounds were golden.
* Not only flat tones are used, but they also play with counterlights to create a sense of depth and volume in the figures.
* Light is not realistic. It generally appears to create volumes or to have symbolic meaning.
* The colors used have symbolic significance.
* The axis of symmetry is taken into account, orienting the elements towards the theoretical center.
* Facial expressions are more exaggerated than in previous periods. A new aesthetic ideal is reflected, leaning towards idealized individual and expressive naturalism.
* The canon features elongated proportions and curvilinear forms. Faces, necks, and hands appear elongated.
* The subject matter is religious, although secular painting also exists.
* Religious themes encompass the life of Jesus, the Virgin Mary, and the saints.
* The purpose is didactic, aimed at teaching something to the viewer.
* Since the works are intended to be viewed up close, they are filled with details.

As the Gothic period progressed, painting became concerned with representing portraits, whether individually or as donors or companions of religious scenes. The reproduction of objects from daily life was included, such as bourgeois scenes inside homes with furniture, paintings, and other objects. There is a fascination with landscapes where the light of the horizon and the reflections on the water are appreciated, and the representations become increasingly realistic, appearing the pictorial space. It is important to note that the end of the Gothic period in painting varied across regions, and the transition to Renaissance styles was not sudden or uniform. Different countries and artists experienced these changes at different times and in unique ways. Nonetheless, the rise of the Renaissance marked a turning point that gradually replaced the dominant characteristics and themes of Gothic painting with new artistic expressions.

Portrait of Giovanni Arnolfini and his wife by the Flemish painter Jan van Eyck. 1,434.

Detail of Descent from the Cross by the Flemish painter Rogier van der Weyden. 1,443.

America, Africa, Asia

America

Pre-Columbian art refers to all forms of art produced before the arrival of the Spanish in the American continent in 1492. The Classical period spans approximately from 200 to 1000 AD, and the Postclassical period covers the years from 1000 to 1500 AD, representing the last 500 years of pre-Columbian art.

Due to invasions, many great works were destroyed, especially those made of gold, as the metal was melted down.

The Postclassical period was characterized by the emergence of military theocracies such as the Mixtecs, Toltecs, and Aztecs.

Sculpture art was grand and massive, often accompanied by a cruel and unsettling expression.

Craftsmanship flourished during the Postclassical period, particularly after learning metalworking techniques for gold, silver, and copper, which were used to create jewelry and ornaments.

Mayan ceramics developed two styles: Mazapan, with a decoration of parallel wavy lines in red and white, and Plumbate, a black ceramic known for its durability and shine.

Atlantes de Tula, an example of post-classic pre-Columbian sculpture. Toltec art.

Africa

Northern regions of Africa followed influences from Europe, such as Christianity and later Islam. In contrast, sub-Saharan Africa remained isolated. The early artistic expressions of these peoples were made with perishable materials and did not survive over time.

In present-day Mali, the Tellem and Dogon peoples developed wood carving.

In West and Southern Africa, bronze objects dating back to the 10th century were produced, as well as certain vessels from the Igbo-Ukwu people in present-day Nigeria. In Nigeria, the Yoruba people emerged in the 12th and 13th centuries and developed a notable school of terracotta figures. In Ethiopia, the rock-hewn churches of Lalibela are remarkable.

Yonghegong Temple. 1694.

Asia

Art in the Asian continent continued to evolve from previous periods. During the Song Dynasty, China developed woodblock printing, ink on silk or paper. The construction of pagodas continued during the Yuan Dynasty, carpets were manufactured, and painting was influenced by religious themes, particularly Taoist and Buddhist. Notable references include the mural paintings of the Yonglegong Temple. Artists such as Huang Gongwang, Wang Meng, and Ni Zan were prominent masters of this era.

By the late Middle Ages, there was a golden age of music. Emperor Xuanzong (Emperor Ming of Tang, who reigned from 712 to 756 AD) had an orchestra with up to 1,300 musicians. He was known for his support of the arts and culture.

Sources

ArtCyclopedia.com Gothic art, Artists by Movement: Gothic Art. Agosto 23, 2007.

Carles Mancho i Suárez. Historia del arte medieval (Educació. Sèrie Materials). Publicacions de la Universidad de València; Edición: 1. 2012.

Carlos Javier Taranilla De La Varga. Breve historia del arte (Nowtilus). Nowtilus; Edición: 1. 2014.

Cennino Cennini. El libro del arte. Editorial Maxtor. 26 de febrero de 2008.

DK. Arte: La historia visual definitiva. DK; Edición: 001. 4 de abril de 2019.

DK. El Libro del Arte (Grandes ideas, Explicaciones Sencillas / Big Ideas Simply Explained). DK. 2017.

Enciclopedia Británica. Gothic art and Gothic era, from "A World History of Art". Agosto 23, 2007.

E.H. Gombrich. La Historia Del Arte. Phaidon; Edición: 16. 2013.

Frederick Hartt. Art: A History of Painting, Sculpture, Architecture. New York: Harry N. Abrams, Inc., 1989.

Isidro Bango Torviso, Gonzalo M. Borrás Gualis, Joaquín Yarza Luaces. Historia del arte. 2. La Edad Media (Libros Singulares (Ls)). Alianza. 1996.

Jesse Bryant Wilder. Historia del arte para Dummies. Para Dummies. 9 de mayo de 2017.

José Alcina Franch, Ignacio Barandiarán. Historia del arte. 1. El Mundo Antiguo (Libros Singulares (Ls)). Alianza; Edición: edición. 4 de octubre de 2004.

Helen Gardner. Art Through the Ages, Sixth Edition, Harcourt Brace Jovanovich, Inc. 1975.

Horst Woldemar Janson. A Short History of Art. 1962.

Lorenzo de la Plaza Escudero. José María Martínez Murillo. Diccionario visual de términos de arte (Arte Grandes Temas). Catedra; Edición: edición. 2015.

Manuel Jesús Roldán Salgueiro. Eso no estaba en mi libro de Historia del Arte. ALMUB|#ALMUZARA; Edición: 1. 2017.

María Carla Prette, Alfonso De Giorgis. Atlas Ilustrado De La Historia Del Arte. Tikal-Susaeta; Edición: Illustrated. 23 de julio de 2004.

Metropolitan Museum of Art Gothic Art and Origin Timeline of Art History. Agosto 2, 2007.

Museen Schleswig-Holstein Gothic art, Museumsportal Government of Schleswig-Holstein. Agosto 23, 2007

Susaeta Ediciones S A. Historia Universal Del Arte. Tikal-Susaeta. 2008.

Yayo Aznar Almazán. Introducción a la Historia del Arte (Manuales). Editorial Universitaria Ramón Areces; Edición: 1. 2014.

Made in United States
Troutdale, OR
11/26/2023